eBooks for Business

Julia A. Royston

B|K
ROYSTON
Publishing

BK Royston Publishing
P. O. Box 4321
Jeffersonville, IN 47131
502-802-5385
http://www.bkroystonpublishing.com
bkroystonpublishing@gmail.com

Cover Design: Richetta Blackmon for
Virtually Splendid –
virtuallysplendid@gmail.com

ISBN-10: 1-946111-20-1
ISBN-13: 978-1-946111-20-3

Printed in the United States of America

Dedication

I dedicate this book to anyone who has a business and wants another product to be more profitable. This book is for you!

Acknowledgement

First, I acknowledge my Lord and Savior Jesus Christ for giving me all of my gifts and especially my gift to write His words.

My husband who is always supportive, loving and encouraging me to utilize all of my gifts and talents. Thank you honey.

To my mother, Dr. Daisy Foree, who is my number one cheerleader and always tells me, "hang in there, you can do it." To my father, Dr. Jack Foree, who is never far away from me in my spirit or heart. I only have to look in the mirror each day to see him.

To Rev. Claude and Mrs. Lillie Royston who support me in everything I do. Especially, Rev. Royston for his careful eye to detail and his sensitive heart to content.

To the rest of my family, I love you and thank you for your prayers, support and love.

To my great friend Vanessa Collins who is always encouraging me to write and try new things in my business. Thanks for being there with me every step of the way. God brought into my life for such a time as this. Love you.

To my business Coach, Dawniel P. Winningham, who has challenged me to be better, go further and do more than I ever thought I would in business.

To my community of authors, graphic designers and future publishers, let's go!

Julia Royston

Table of Contents

Introduction

So you're in business and so many have been telling you that you need a book including me. Why? The next few pages are going to tell you why you need an eBook in your Business.

I will tell you that I have written more than 35 books and excited to share my tips, tricks and talent with you on writing your first of many eBooks.

As a publisher, I believe that everyone should write, publish and promote a book. It gives you a voice, showcases your expertise and you now have a product to sell. If you own a business, have a career or a professional in any capacity, you should have a book. As a publisher who has been in business for nearly 10 years, I've seen my share of manuscripts, met and worked with many authors as well as provided information to many others. I have seen the benefit of a book to someone's business if you take it seriously, write the right book and incorporate it into your business life.

This book will assist you in writing the right book, knowing your publishing and promotional options as well as explore the potential of your book to the future growth, expansion and platform of your business.

Now, before we get started let me tell you that my company is here to help you complete and not just to start your book. If you get stuck, have a problem or a question related to writing a book, don't hesitate to reach out to me at www.bkroystonpublishing.com or email us at bkroystonpublishing@gmail.com or call 502-802-5385. We'll be happy to help.

Also visit http://bit.ly/roystonebooks for more resources, worksheets and other opportunities to be helped by the staff of BK Royston Publishing and Julia Royston Enterprises.

There is another resource to help writers and that is the Write. Publish. Promote Series from Julia Royston. To obtain your copy of this series, visit:

Http://www.writepublishpromoteitnow.com

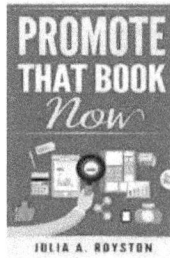

We have wasted enough time dreaming, hoping and believing to be a published author. Turn the page to get started writing that "eBook for Your Business!" Let's go!

Julia Royston

Chapter 1

Why an eBook?

An eBook is high in demand. There are still people that want the book in paper format, and I believe that you should have it in paper and the eBook format. Technology has helped to fuel the growing demand for the eBook. The capabilities of the phone and its abilities has revolutionized the way that we communicate, do business and get information. Our current connection with the phone is unparalleled with any other technological device, and eBooks can be delivered directly to your phone. Not to mention, all of the eReaders that are being created and then add the ability to electronically download the digital files directly to the audience either for free or for a fee. The distribution of the eBook will be discussed much later, but it has to be a major consideration when writing it. So society is asking, "Why can't I have the book on my phone, laptop, tablet, NOOK reader, kindle and desktop to read anytime and anywhere I want?" You don't have to carry around a book because all of your mobile devices have the capability of having that same book in it. It's what I like to call the 'convenience factor.' The convenience factor is to make it is as easy as possible for customer to get access to your information, product or service. Stop the excuses up front by having your content available in all formats including the eBook to make it easier, convenient, affordable and as accessible as possible. We live in a 'drive through or click through' society where we can get our food quickly and easily and the desire to get information in a matter of clicks and download is even more desirable as well. It's incredible.

As a print and digital publisher, there are so many things that don't have to be done or considered when publishing an eBook. First, there is no page limit. You can have as few or as many pages as you want. You must have a certain amount of pages for the printer to print your book in its physical format. Second, the layout and formatting for a digital book is much easier and requires less work, once the book has been edited. Third, there is no layout of the book cover because only the front of the book cover is used in eBooks. There is no printing cost with an eBook. There is no delivery fee, shipping or package handling fee with the eBook. A digital book is not delivered through the U. S. Postal Service or another delivery service. We are moving or transferring or downloading the book electronically. Therefore, the book can be delivered globally with the major online distribution companies. You have the ability to have your book delivered through distribution outlets that were off limits to independent or smaller publishing houses just a few years ago.

On the other hand, there are some countries that some distribution companies have limited access to for the print book and shipping limitations. There are restrictions on what can be brought into certain countries. With an eBook, that limitation is removed. There will be a distribution fee with the online distribution companies but it's all digitally transferred. The eBook is here to stay and growing in popularity every day.

So why an eBook? The audience wants it, the technology is there to give the audience the accessibility and the convenience of the delivery of the book makes it a win, win. So why not an eBook? You have the content in your head. You know what your clients, customers and audience needs. Write it down and let's get it to the people. The old say, "give the people what they want" in an eBook.

If you need help with your eBook, don't hesitate to reach out to me via email at julia@bkroystonpublishing.com or call 502-802-5385.

Julia A. Royston

_____

_____

_____

_____

_____

_____

_____

_____

_____

_____

_____

_____

_____

_____

_____

_____

_____

_____

_____

_____

_____

_____

_____

_____

_____

Chapter 2

What does it mean to my business?

I have something else to sell. The first thing that the eBook does for your business is that it is an additional product added to your existing product line in whatever business that you are currently in. You now have something else to sell and profit from. Remember the more products you have to sell, the likelihood of being more profitable is more obtainable. After the eBook is finished, tell yourself, "I now have something else to sell." Whether you are in the beauty, publishing, law or medical field, an eBook is another product to sell.

Credibility and My Voice

Your eBook is adding credibility to you as an expert, author and a person in the field or industry in which you engage and transact business. Additionally, your eBook is positioning you as an expert in the particular field or industry. Your voice, opinion and stance on the issues, standards, products, procedures, methods and services of your industry, can now be heard and expressed through your eBook. With your expertise on this subject, your book gives your expertise a voice. You can now be recognized as an expert in the field and relied upon as a resource, authority and reference in your business' industry. You have an opinion, stance and information regarding a topic.

With the search engines of the large online distribution company websites, if someone did a search on your industry area, topic of discussion or expertise, your book should come up on the list. You should be able to find your book, and then with a little more searching find out about you.

I recently had a couple write a book on a topic that is very necessary and desired. With a very simple topical search, their book show up on Amazon.com on the first page. That is important for people to be able to find your book in your subject area quickly and easily. For their particular book and subject area, they show up on the first page of the search results. Without much promotion or driving traffic, people who search on that topic should be able to find the book and hopefully, there is a great possibility of them buying the book because they could find it easily.

You know that companies traditionally put the bestselling, most demanded products or just on sale items at the counter when you are about to check out because in sight, you may buy it too. The same marketing strategy should be utilized electronically with your eBook. It should be noticed, upfront and easy to find which will lead to your voice to be heard by millions just like anyone in the field.

Platform Building

Your eBook should be the wood, nails and glue that is the foundation for building your platform. Your eBook is a product, gives you credibility, your thoughts a voice, but also should be a part of the platform you stand on. No matter if your eBook highlights a new discovery, dispels myths or disregards the normal and take the traditional in a new direction that is all involved in building a platform. Once your book is done, you should start speaking about the topic of your book. Once people hear what you have to say, they will purchase your book and continue to refer you, recognize you for your expertise and knowledge and then continue to return to you for more content related to your business and eBook topic.

When I first began in the publishing business/industry, I was only publishing my books and had one other author that I had published. The author was happy with the results of her book. The book sold well but I only had some experience with publishing. Now after 9 ½ years, 100+ books published and more than 55 authors signed to my company, I now have a reputation in my city, state, across the country and internationally for publishing books People call me, refer me and want to work with me to help them publish their books. My experience, patience and reputation now have helped build my platform in the publishing industry. Your experience, expertise and eBook should be helping to build your platform, express your voice, expand your reach and influence others. The more people know about your business. The more people that experience your voice and expertise, the more people will want to do business with you and buy your book. What's your industry? What's your business? You should be striving daily to build, bring attention and grow your business. You should be a spokesperson for your industry, business, market and book. Your eBook should be one of the tools you use for helping and moving that process more rapidly. The more you speak, the more you travel, the more you are interviewed, the more you are exposed to the world, the more popular you become and the more in demand you, your books and your services will become.

Stream of Income

Your book is a stream of income. When you sell it, you profit from it. The eBook can also be an accompanying stream of income along with other products and services. Ever heard of bundling? Sure, the phone industry is great at it, but this marketing tactic shouldn't be limited to the phone industry. Your eBook can be the book, workbook or guide for a workshop, online course, webinar, coaching, conference or retreat. The possibilities are endless barring that the book is on a topic related to or essential to your business. Can you say, "Money is coming to me?" With your eBook, "money is coming to you?"

If you need help with your eBook, don't hesitate to reach out to me via email at julia@bkroystonpublishing.com or call 502-802-5385.

Julia A. Royston

_____

_____

_____

_____

_____

_____

_____

_____

_____

_____

_____

_____

_____

_____

_____

_____

_____

_____

_____

_____

Chapter 3

Let's get started.

One thing about eBooks for business is that it is focused on topics about business, related to your business or for other business owners. There may be other genres of books that you want to write about. I write in multiple genres including children's, romantic fiction, inspirational and poetry but for our study today, it's all about our business. This book will focus on your business industry, business platform, business market, sales, products, services, growth tactics or profitability methods. Whatever will help grow a business in your industry area should be related to or a part of your eBook for business. You should have an interest in this topic. You should be passionate about your business, what you do and how you impact the lives of others that this eBook should literally flow out of you like this book is flowing out of me. Just as a side note, don't choose a business that you have no interest in. This could be related to your job that you love but if you choose business, it should be a business that you eat, sleep and dream about. This eBook should be an extension of you and what you do. This eBook should contain your thoughts, ideas and ideals.

Topic

If you don't have a topic to write about then, let's find one. Go to Google and type in "Bestselling books." Find a list of the bestselling books that are currently on the market. This list will help you determine what books people are actually buying. If one of the topics interests you then, decide to write about it. Don't worry about the title or how long your book will be compared to the book that is already published. At this point, we are just trying to determine the topic. You also want to distinguish your book from the books that are out there so, if you decide on a particular popular topic then determine a different angle or approach to the topic.

Also, I caution you to write about a topic that you have a genuine interest in. Remember that once your book is published, you will have to speak about your book as well as remember the title and where to buy it. On the other hand, if the topic you want to write about is a topic on the bestsellers list, you are well on your way to writing a book that not only people want to read but are willing to buy. Once you have decided on a topic, it is now time to begin the writing process.

Over the years, I have developed my own approach to writing books. I have written books purely from inspiration, having an outline with the issues I want to discuss in the book clearly detailed.

My first suggestion is to approach your book with the way that works best for you. If it's not broke, don't fix it. If you get stuck and need help, reach out to a writing coach or someone who has written books before.

For first time authors, I suggest having an outline with the subjects that you want to cover so that it helps with writer's block and the flow of your writing.

The message of the book and the topic of the book are different. The topic of the book is what you want to write about or the genre of the book. Fiction or romance fiction or self-help for domestic violence or even how to fix a sink. These are just some sample topics for a book. Inside the general topic of the book should be a message that you want to deliver to the reader. For example, the topic of the book is "Six Ways to Fix a Sink." The message of the book is that anybody can fix a sink with these simple instructions, step by step images and/or an instructional DVD. In other words, the message of the book should be related to the why of the book or the what? Remember that at the end of a speech, talk, lesson or instruction there should be a reason why you did the talk, taught the lesson or gave the instructions. Why? The message of the book should be that why or the reason for the book being written in the first place. Think about the reason or message of your book. It should connect with you first, because you have to be passionate about and believe in what you are writing. Secondly, there should be someone else in the world who needs that message right now. The reason for my writing this book, 'Write that Book, Now' is because there are billions of people in the world with many diverse needs, problems and situations. Your story, message and book could help them with that problem or situation. That's my message to you, "Write that eBook for Your Business Now!" Let's go!

Outline it.

The outline is the framework, guide and pathway to the completion of your book. The outline helps you stay on course and not detour off into to unnecessary subjects of this particular book. The topics that you don't use or discuss in this book can be used for another book. The outline you are creating should cover the topics that you want to discuss in your book. It's plain and simple. The topics do not have to be in final order or level of importance. The importance of the outline is to have a focus for the book, and if there are more issues surrounding the topic that are not included in the first outline then those issues could be for future books. Your book needs to have a focused topic but under that topic should be the points or message that you wish to deliver. These should all be the determined in the outline.

You can write down the outline on paper. Others have suggested putting each topic on a note card. I sit down at a computer and begin writing my outline. Each line of my document should point to the one topic that I want to discuss.

For example, if your book was about 10 ways to be happy, the outline could look like the following:

Topic: 10 Ways to Be Happy

Happiness Definition

Life

Family

Health

Success

Business

Freedom

Now, before I give someone an idea for a best-selling book, I will stop at the above list of potential topics. The outline above is not in a particular order but clearly lists the topics that I, the author, would deem important, in my opinion, for happiness. With this outline, underneath each topic, begin writing about the topics on the outline. So, first, what is the definition of happiness? Second, what about your life would bring happiness? Third, what about family could or would make you happy?

You are writing your book based on the outline and filling in the blanks of the text under each topic. It's just that simple.

An outline is a great guide and map to writing your book. Once you are finished filling in the blanks or writing the text under your outline topics, go back and read what you have written. It will surprise you how much you have written. These topics can now be transposed into chapter titles. You could leave the chapter titles as simple one word headings or adjust them to longer sentences. It is your choice.

The outline can be directed at a customer to answer their questions concerning your business and what you offer. Secondly, your eBook could be directed at someone new to the industry or finally, someone who has been in the industry a while and needs to improve their skills.

Write it.

Audience

Approach

Tone

Book Connection

Business Tool/Resource Use

You have the outline and should begin writing the manuscript immediately once the outline is developed and determined. If you are like me, you enjoy writing and don't find it hard to find the time or effort to write. Everyone is not the same, and it may be your first book and your first attempt at writing a book. Here are some helpful hints for writing your book.

Schedule Time

Schedule time to write each day. Look at your weekly schedule. Determine when you get up, have to be at work and what your evenings look like. When do you have the most time to write? Is it in the morning when you wake up or in the evening before you go to bed? If I am focused on a topic, I write whenever I have free time, morning, noon and night. For you and your life, it might not be that easy. You decide but get to a time, schedule each day and stick to it. The book won't write itself so, you have to approach it like any other task. Make time for it. You make time for everything else and this is no different.

It has been suggested that you write for periods of time and then take breaks. These breaks cause you to walk away from the manuscript, rest your mind and body so that you can be more productive when you return to your manuscript. However, you do it, just do it. Write until you finish the book. The bottom line of finishing the book is to write.

Get an accountability partner

Tell someone that you are writing a book and let them hold you accountable for it. Get out your calendar and schedule times and days to check in with this person. Tell them your frustrations and possible delays in getting the book done. Let them motivate you and help you get the book done. You may even have to reach out to a professional book writing coach or mentor to help you stay committed to the process. That's what Julia Royston Enterprises does. They help authors get started and keep moving forward until they achieve the end result of being a published author. Reach out to someone who has actually written a book. They know the process intimately and can offer suggestions to help you keep going until you finish. No matter how long it takes, keep going until you finish. There is someone waiting on your book. Don't stop until you are done!

Commitment and Determination

As with any undertaking, there must be a level of commitment, determination and dedication to getting it done. There should be a sense of pride, courage, wisdom and faith in what you are attempting. No matter what that project is, there will be distractions, physical tiredness, possible writer's block, family crisis and financial delays, but be determined to get it done. I've had writers reach out to me who have wanted to publish a book for more than 40 years. I know why they haven't done it yet and that's because they weren't committed to doing it in the past but because so much time has passed, they now realize that they don't know how much longer they will live, so they are more focused now than ever. Put in the work, stay committed to anything and you will reap the rewards for your efforts.

Writing is Emotional

Your thoughts, feelings, pain, joys and experiences can and may be included in your book. Time after time, I have had authors tell me of the emotional roller coaster ride that they have been on while writing their book. The autobiographical genre brings out the hidden, deep, dark and sometimes extremely painful experiences in a person's life. I have had authors stop writing because they didn't want to face the past. But, I have encouraged them that they can't overcome what they won't face. Some of you might ask, I thought she was a publisher? I am but writing is emotional. Writing brings up emotions, and situations from the past that you thought you had conquered only to have them be revisited and realize that the pain hasn't fully gone away. Remember that someone else has and is experiencing that same pain. Your ability to live past your pain could be a message that someone needs to hear, so that they can get past theirs as well. Writing is therapeutic and directly tied to your emotional well-being. Writer heal thyself through your writing. Keep writing.

Re-Writes

Re-writing is a critical phase after the first draft and should be seen with fresh eyes after the rough draft is finished. I find that reading a manuscript after I have put it away for a few days really allows me to be ready to do the re-writes. In the re-writes, your focus is to not start the book from scratch but to add any missing pieces or any other things that you want to say. Don't remove anything unless it does not follow the outline or isn't pertinent to the book. Don't delete it permanently, because it could be the idea or important piece to another book, but shouldn't be included in this first book. When you are finished with the re-writes, let it go to someone else. Let someone you trust read it to make sure that it makes sense to them, and the message you were trying to get across was delivered. If not clear, ask them what was not clear and make the change. It is that simple. Just make the message clearer; don't delete or throw away the book. Criticism comes with the territory of writing. Don't let your emotions stop or block you from creating and delivering the best book possible.

You put your feelings into the book, but don't let your feelings stop you from moving forward to finish the book. I am the first to admit, that I am sensitive about everything I create and want people to like it as much as I do. But at the end of the day, people still have to be able to understand what you wrote even if they don't agree. That is the beauty of writing. It is not that people have to agree, but they do have to understand and get the clear picture of what you were trying to say in the book. There are books out there that are very controversial and do well selling in the marketplace. But a poorly written book is just that, a poorly written book, no matter the topic.

Finish the Book!

Whether on a napkin, paper, tissue, computer or journal notebook, just write. No matter when you write, just write. There is no other way around it; just write and finish the book.

No matter how long it takes or what you need to finish, just finish it. Whether it takes six months or six years, finish the book.

Get the heart of a finisher and finish the book. There is nothing like finishing any project. But when your book is finished, published and it is available online or maybe it will land on a bookshelf, there is nothing like it.

Don't wait another minute! Don't delay another day! Write and Finish!

If you need help finishing or writing your eBook, don't hesitate to reach out to me via email at julia@bkroystonpublishing.com or call 502-802-5385.

Julia A. Royston

_____

_____

_____

_____

_____

_____

_____

_____

_____

_____

_____

_____

_____

_____

_____

_____

_____

_____

_____

_____

_____

_____

_____

Chapter 4

Publishing the eBook

What is Publishing?

Publishing is defined as 'to issue (printed or otherwise reproduced textual or graphic material, computer software, etc.) for sale or distribution to the public or the activities of a publisher to get a book or periodical prepared for sale or distribution.' (dictionary.com)

You may not see yourself as a publisher, but you are. You are the author and the publisher simultaneously. You have put your thoughts on paper, you are preparing the manuscript and will soon select a distribution outlet for your book. You are doing what it takes to get that book to be distributed and sold. So let's get that manuscript prepared for distribution and sale.

Rough Draft

First, a rough draft is just that rough. If you opened the manuscript in Microsoft Word, you should see red lines, green and blue lines of errors. That is fine because remember the book is rough.

Next, do the basic editing of Microsoft Office or even Google Docs Spell Check. Check for basic spelling errors or grammatical errors that the system catches and make those corrections quickly. Resave the document, close the document and don't look at it for 3-5 days. Yes, I said put it away for 3-5 days. Why? Because when you see the document again, you will need fresh eyes to properly review it again. You know what you meant to say and if you try to make that change now you won't catch it and overlook it. Thus, the reason for putting the manuscript in its current state away. You will read other things, watch television, listen to music, go to work and go to sleep, which are things unrelated to your book. This should clear your mind and readers pallet, so that you can look at the book with fresh eyes and be more critical of what you are seeing. The next stage is self-editing and maybe more re-writes.

Editing the eBook

I am not an advocate at all of self-editing the final book. It is just not wise. Your eyes, mind and the words play tricks on each other. You know what you wanted to say, but don't have it on the page at all. I will always have an editor no matter what. You need other eyes to read it, comprehend it without you and give their feedback on what they are reading. The person reading it needs to know that it makes sense to them.

Prior to even getting another person to read it, another technique is to read the manuscript out loud. Don't read it to yourself because that will keep you in the tricky area instead of in the real truth of what is written. Your ears and your mouth will help you determine if what you meant to say was actually what was on the paper.

The main benefit of reading it out loud is to catch mistakes on the first time. Once you have made changes from reading it out loud the first time, press record. If you have recording software or app, once you finish reading it the second time, you now have a recording of it. You can record the whole book or the first two chapters as a teaser for the audience. It can help with promotion of the book later. What an idea!

I wrote this book that way. I recorded the book first and then wrote down what I recorded. Of course, you can add things as you go but it sure is quicker having a recording already done and can transcribe the recording instead of writing from scratch and then recording again.

Now your book has gone from rough draft through at least 2 re-writes and maybe been recorded. You have hopefully done some correcting to the manuscript and ready to turn it over to someone else.

Next, ask a friend, neighbor, former English teacher or another person who is very observant and critical with the written word. It will amaze the things that people will ask that you never thought of while writing the book. Ask them their opinion, if anything wasn't clear and then what they thought of the book. Your future readers will not have the benefit of you sitting next to them while they read your book to explain any parts that they don't understand or doesn't make sense. To avoid this, the person that you select to read the book for clarity and understanding is help to this part for you. Be brave and trust them because in the end, it is helping you and your book.

You now have your first review of the book. As them if you can use their comments in publicity but it is a comment, review or response to reading the book just the same. After their comments, make some more changes. Next, I always advise you to hire a professional editor or reviewer. Now, you may know a professor that is head of the university's English Department that will edit it for you but just in case, hire a professional. Once the professional has reviewed your book, they will either make the corrections for you or you will have to make the corrections based on their suggestions but make those corrections quickly. Save your document often and in multiple places. You have invested a lot of time, effort and money into this book, so don't lose it.

If you need help with the editing or questions about the storage of your book, don't hesitate to reach out to BK Royston Publishing at julia@bkroystonpublishing.com or call us at 502-802-5385.

Formatting the eBook

The basic formatting of an eBook is different that a regular paperback book. First it should be laid out in an 8 1/2 x 11 format. There are 4 file formats for an eBook to be distributed digitally. The first is a Microsoft Word file format or a file that ends in .docx or .doc. This file format can be used for multiple digital outlets for your book. Because of the smaller screens of the eReaders, the title page font should be no larger than 18 or 24 font size. Much larger than that and it won't show up clearly on the screen.

Each section or chapter of the book should start on a new page. Therefore, the title page should start on its own page, the copyright page, then the dedication page and so on. Each chapter should start on its own new page. You won't be reading the book like a paperback, so the book can just flow from one page to the next without the worry of which side of the page are you starting the chapter or section of the book.

If you have chapter titles, center and bold them if you like, so that they will stand out a little more. Don't worry about headers and footers because of the different sizes of the eReaders you don't know where they will start or stop so leave them out altogether. The eBook is not based or limited to the amount of pages or the margins, etc. like the paperback book. Make sure that the content of the book is high quality and that it has been edited properly. The order of the book is similar to the order of the pages for a paperback book.

Order of Pages for the Book

There is a standard order of pages and content that the reader will be looking for when they open your book. This is called the format or layout of the book. Below you will find the correct order of the pages that should be included in your book. If you don't have the pages in this order then you will have to develop those pages and put them in the correct order.

The Front Pages of the book

The front pages of the book are the pages in the beginning of the book directly after the cover. I encourage you to browse through published books to get an idea of what you like and what you want your book to look like once it is published.

The front pages include the title page, copyright page, dedication, acknowledgement, foreword (if desired), table of contents as well as an introduction of the book. The manuscript of the book should follow after the introduction, foreword or preface of the book.

An ISBN number is not required for KINDLE or NOOK eBooks. The Canadian KOBO eReader does offer or prefer eISBN for their manuscript submissions.

The eBook can be formatted as a .pdf, .docx, .epub or .mobi file.

Cover of the Book

I cannot tell you how important the cover of a book is to its success. I often go back and forth when it comes to deciding between whether the outside or the inside of the book is the most important. They are both very important, but the inside of the book will rarely be seen if the outside of the book is not appealing and does not clearly represent the inside of the book and its message.

A book may be a number one bestseller, but if the cover is not appealing then people won't buy it. That is often the reason why when authors change the book cover, the book starts to sell. The author may not have changed one single word on the inside but when the cover changed, the sells changed. I am a living witness to this fact and willing to be transparent to tell you that. A new cover has actually revitalized and reintroduced my book to a new audience based on the cover and then the contents.

For the eBook, you only need the front cover of the book. Unless you intend to print the book later, the spine or back of the book is not necessary. You do need a teaser or short description of the book to be placed on the online distribution outlets. Additionally, you will need a short bio of the author for the eBook as well. It is not required but I always highly recommend it. The teaser and bio of the author are included in the online distribution sites such as Amazon.com or Barnes&Noble.com.

If you need help preparing your eBook for publishing, don't hesitate to reach out to me via email at julia@bkroystonpublishing.com or call 502-802-5385.

Chapter 5

Publishing Options

There are multiple publishing options and outlets available today with technology and the global reach of the Internet to publish your book. A few options to consider. First, publish it to your own website. You can save the document as a .pdf formatted file and just provide it for sale on your own website or ecommerce store. It is easy quick and you do not share the profits for distribution with anyone. The objective would be to have a marketing and promotional team to drive people to your website to purchase the book. There is no shipping because it is an eBook. There is no handling because it is totally digital downloading. You should have a way to collect the email addresses of your customer, collect the payment through a payment system which we will discuss in a minute and you now are generating a stream of income through the sale of your book. Easy right? In theory it is easy but it is hard work and time consuming to drive that traffic to your website. Wouldn't it be better for your book to be available on multiple outlets rather than just one? The more outlets that the book is available, the more people will have the options to purchase your book. There are people who only have a KINDLE or NOOK or KOBO or want to have it downloaded directly to their computer. The greater the options, the greater the opportunity to reach more people have make more sales.

With that being said, let's explore more options. KINDLE eReader is owned by Amazon. Amazon.com is one of the largest if not the largest online distributor in the world. The literally have millions of credit cards on file and a search engine capability on their website that can not only search in English but multiple languages to attract people around the globe.

In my mind, that is incredible. Now, there is a fee to have the distribution ability but why wouldn't you want that? You can continue to drive traffic to your website but also don't miss out on the millions people who already visit Amazon each and every day.

NOOK is an eReader from Barnes&Noble.com which is no small operation as well. The ability to have a presence on the Barnes&Noble.com NOOK website is fantastic and creates another distribution outlet for your eBook.

KOBO is a Canadian eReader that exposes your book to another English speaking audience. Additionally, if your eBook was only available through KINDLE or NOOK, you would miss out on this audience altogether not having your eBook on their service. There is a fee for this distribution but isn't it worth it? If someone wanted to place a book or any other merchandise on your website, wouldn't you charge for their space on your site? The same is true with all of these distribution outlets. It's just business.

Publishing Timeline and Payments

The faster the book is available for sale and the links to your payment system are in place, the faster you will start making money. The timeline for publishing is left up to you. Because you don't have to wait on a printer, shipping, etc. for an eBook like you do for the paperback, you can set the publishing timeline initially. If the book is written and formatted today, you can have it upload to your website today and available for sell the same day. There is no wait on your own site. You should have control of your own site.

If you choose to upload your book to KINDLE, NOOK or KOBO which you should to all three systems, the book up will be available to sell within 24-48 hours. If you upload the file to all 4 systems, you have the potential to have 4 publishing outlets that have your book available. Thus, when you put together your advertisement for your book, you should have those distribution outlet logos on your flyer or social media posts for the convenience of your audience to buy your book.

In the past, receiving payments was different. The most you had to worry about was having change for cash. Today, we live in a digital currency and not as much cash and in the days gone by. I rarely have cash on me. It is better for business record keeping as well to have an electronic/digital transaction. Now, my business will accept cash but what about those people like me who don't carry cash at all. Be ready. When I first started accepting credit cards, I had the bulky swiper, carbon copy slips to keep track of and had to mail the slips to the company and then wait on my money to arrive.

Now, I can swipe a credit card, have the approval of the funds and the money is on the way to my account in a matter of minutes. I use several different merchant accounts, because I have done business internationally and some credit card companies, including PayPal don't accept some credit cards from certain countries.

I use multiple credit card merchant institutions including PayPal, Stripe, Square and my own merchant account with my business bank account. I want to be able to accept payments from multiple sources and not miss out on a sale or leave money on the table for my products and services. After 9 ½ years in business, I have to be ready at all times. People buy books anywhere and anytime they see me. I have my phone with the appropriate app, charged and ready to take payments at live events, online as well as the grocery story if people want to buy my books.

The average fee from the credit card company is 2.9%. That leaves you 97.3% of the funds for you and your business. I will take the 97.3% over nothing. I realize that some people want to find an excuse to say no, but I eliminate all excuses if at all possible.

Don't let the lack of payment options stop you from the sale. Make sure that you have your publishing and payment options in order to build your wealth with your words.

If you have any questions or need additional information about editing, formatting, publishing or payments, reach out at julia@bkroystonpublishing.com, call 502-802-5385 or visit http://bit.ly/roystonebooks.

Chapter 6

What is Promotion?

Promotion is defined as something devised to publicize or advertise a product, cause, institution, etc. Something such as a brochure, free sample, poster, television or radio commercial, or personal appearance (dictionary.com)

Promotion; to me, is using any means necessary to get the attention of a buyer of your product or service. Whatever it takes to get people's attention and encourages them to buy your product is what should be used.

Once your book is written and published, promotion is the hardest and most important part of the process prior to selling the book.

I will discuss methods that I have used personally or have seen my authors use as a proven method to promote and launch your book.

Before you even begin the promotion process, you need to realize that it is going to take hard work and consistency. You will sell to some people as soon as the book is released and available. This is wonderful. But to have long term sales or expose your book to new customers, then it will take every means possible to promote your book.

Most new authors give up on the promotion and sales process right after the initial book signing, and that is a mistake. Why? Because there are billions of people on earth who have not heard of your book yet. How will they know about your book if you stop promoting after the initial book release or virtual book launch? There are literally millions of books being published every year. Sure, there will be people who will not be interested in your book and that is fine. But, what about the people who are interested, but do not have the opportunity to read your book because you stopped promoting.

One question that I ask all authors that I coach or publish is if they are ready? You may think, 'ready for what?' And I'm glad that you asked. Are you ready for your life to change after you publish and promote your book? If you are really serious about selling and promoting your book, then things in your life will have to change.

First, you will now be a published author. You will have added a new position and title to your name and life. Second, you will now be in the business of writing. And finally, you will be a representative and promoter of a product.

You should now be seeking ways and opportunities to promote and sell your book. Promotion and sales and the ability to transact currency all go together. Promoting a product without an outlet to sell it is futile and a waste of your time and effort.

If you are like me and not that good at sales, then you will figure it out or otherwise you won't sell books.

The places where you spend your time may have to change, since you will need to spend some time marketing, promoting and selling your book to people with money and an interest in your book.

Promoting takes time and being in the presence of your audience.

Look at your life and see ways, places and people that may have to change in order to properly promote and sell your book.

We will look at the Pre-Launch, Active Launch and Post Launch process.

Pre-Launch

Pre-Orders are a way to receive income prior to the book's release, gain interest surrounding your book and gauge how many books will be sold. Pre-orders are also a way to promote your book. The instant that you reveal your book cover to the world, social media or to a close friend, you have begun your promotional efforts. Pre-orders bring in income but pre-orders can also be a part of the promotional process.

Pre-sales or pre-orders work best when you are sure that the book is finished and have a guaranteed time that the book will be finished. With the eBook, there is a time limit for pre-orders in KINDLE and when the book is available, the book is downloaded directly to the person KINDLE. You will also receive the profit/royalty from the pre-order prior to the actual book's release. If you have more questions or need help with pre-orders, don't hesitate to reach out via email at julia@bkroystonpublishing.com or call 502-802-5385.

Prior to launching any new product or service, you have to make sure that the distribution outlets, links to payment processing and delivery system for your book is in place. If your book is distributed on KINDLE, NOOK or KOBO that is taken place all on their website. Once the book is uploaded and the information about the book listed, those services review the book to make sure that it meets their standards and then the book is live and available for sale. They take care of delivering your eBook to their eReaders and you collect the royalties.

Next, who are your followers on Facebook? How many people are on your email list? Who do you network with locally that would have an interest in your book? Who are your clients or customers? You need to do an inventory of people that would have an interest in your book and hopefully, buy it.

Build, Engage and Connect

It is so much harder to sell a book without a social media presence, list or a network. I encourage authors that throughout the writing process, you maintain and grow a social media presence by post regularly. You should not just start posting to social media to sell your book. You will be greatly disappointed. Have you supported anyone else's book signing, product, service, event, conference or workshop? Do you share other people's posts and help them advertise their products, services or events? If not, look for very little help for you. Additionally, there is no guarantee that people will support you when you do support them so network to help your cause rather than hinder it.

Posting consistently is just as important as what you post on social media. Post a picture of your cover as a teaser and introduction to what the book cover is going to look like so that people will be on the lookout for the book.

Post very short excerpts from the book which should include a quote, idea or strong point that you are going to be making inside the book itself.

Video

In additional to social media posting is video. Live Stream or short videos are worth 10,000 words if a picture is worth 1,000 words. That picture of your very well done cover is going to get a lot reaction. But when you do a short streaming video of engaging content, there should be even more reaction and engagement to your post.

Active Launch

An eBook launch is different than a regular physical book launch. A physical book launch can be an event at an actual venue, with food or other activities. For physical books, you will need to have them printed and reviewed for any problems or errors, prior to the actual event. With a virtual or eBook launch there are no physical books that have to be purchased, but promotion has to actively take place to lead, guide and prompt people to the website to where you are hosting and distributing your eBook.

You should have professionally created graphics, banners or flyers complete with your professional photo not bathroom selfies, posted on all of your social media and other promotional outlets. You should schedule an online event encouraging people to purchase your eBook, especially on Amazon.com, during a specific scheduled time period for improved ranking and hopefully, a top 10 ranking for the downloads of your book. You should have a team watching the rankings, sharing your posts and encouraging people to purchase your book during the book launch event. In addition, you should try to find people that will gift a book or 10 to other people. You could provide gift cards for people to purchase or gift books to others, but you didn't hear that from me.

Promotional Outlets

Here are some promotional outlets to help draw attention to your eBook.

Amazon Author Central - Amazon provides an Author page for people that have books available for purchase on their website. Be sure and complete the Amazon Author Central which is a free service. The Amazon Author Central page is complete with links to your blog, website, a video and can list all of the books that you have available for purchase on Amazon.com. If you don't have a website built, this is one place to start.

Website - We discussed earlier about publishing your eBook to your website. You can't publish an eBook to the site if you don't have a website. There are all type of website building software out there. Investigate it, do your homework, build the site and then promote it and have your book located on that site for the world to see.

Blog - A blog can be used for posting and as a website. Consider using some of the larger blogging sites such as WordPress, Blogger, etc.

Social Media - Social Media is a no brainer and one of the first places to promote your eBook, virtual book launch event and provide excerpts from your book to draw people in to buy it.

Advertising - No matter how much free advertisements and opportunities you utilize, there will be times and places that you will not gain access or preferential treatment to some audiences unless you pay. Whether you advertise in the paper, a newsletter, a conference packet, etc. there should be some level of investment.

Press Release - Press Releases still get the attention of the media. It may seem old fashioned, but if you are serious about promoting your book, you'll use any means necessary. There are free or paid services that will circulate your press release for you.

Video - Video is KING right now. If you don't have a YouTube Channel, I don't know why not because it is free. Using Periscope, Facebook LIVE, Instagram Stories, Twitter LIVE and any other method of recording a video is priceless and preferred. So jump in. It doesn't have to be perfect, but you need to be getting your message out there. Let's go!

Live Events - I host live events all of the time whether virtually or in person. I strive to gain exposure for my books and my business by having one of my books be the handout or the guide or the workbook for the event. People like to attend live events to get out of the house, network, meet new people and learn new things. Host a LIVE Event of your own surrounding your topic or the topic of your book. It doesn't have to be very expensive just effective. Always create and compile a list of those that attend this event so that you don't have to start from scratch for the next event.

Speaking Engagements - Books move when you speak. Why? People want to make connection with the author. They don't just want the book that you are selling, but they want to invest in the author of the book.

Give-a-ways - People love give a ways. Give a Ways help draw attention to your book and hopefully, support from others by sharing the offer. Once the offer is shared, the objective achieved, and then others will see the book and want to buy it.

Post Launch

Remain engaged with your audience even after the initial launch of the book. Determine what worked and what didn't work during the launch. Meaning, what did your audience respond to and what didn't they respond to. Finally, whatever worked repeat it and whatever didn't work, try again another time with a different book.

Is promotion not your thing? Do you need ideas and places to promote? I understand. And for more help or guidance on ways to promote your book, reach out to us via email at julia@juliaroystonenterprises.com or call us at 502-802-5385.

_____

_____

_____

_____

_____

_____

_____

_____

_____

_____

_____

_____

_____

_____

_____

_____

_____

_____

_____

_____

_____

_____

_____

Chapter 7

Multi-Purposing and Re-Purposing

In this chapter, I just want to touch on just the few of the many ways that your eBook can be repurposed or multi-purposed.

First, let me define re-purpose or multi-purpose. My definition of re-purpose is that you can take your book or your book's message and it will become the foundation for multiple events, other books or media outlets. For example, this book you are now reading that I have just written is a class already. It is a 4 week boot camp and you can sign up for it at http://bit.ly/roystonebooks. This same book can be the basis for a weekend retreat or intensive summit, webinar or virtual or in-person conference. The ability to take the information in this book and refer to it by a teacher or speaker in a different setting or environment is growth, expansion and an opportunity for multi-use.

Next, this book will never contain or hold all of the ideas that your eBook can be transformed into or re-used for because there will be new ways and ideas to repurpose your book in the future. Here are just a few of the ways or ideas that your book can be used along with or converted into:

Workbook

Course/Class/Workshop

Retreat

Webinar

Intensive Weekend

Conference

Podcast

Live Streaming Event

With just this list of possible uses for your eBook, your business has a great chance of being more profitable than it is already. There is opportunity to have your book or message or business seen by a different audience by just changing the format of your book or message delivery system. Why? Because there are people who won't come to your retreat, but are loyal listeners of podcasts. There are people who will follow you on Live Stream, but may not buy your book until they have seen and heard you live. There are people who love to travel and would attend your retreat, but would not buy your book online. These people will automatically get your book because it will be included in the registration of your retreat, conference or other live event.

These are just a few of the reasons why all businesses need a book. Yes, I am in the publishing business, and books are my thing.

But finding ways to make your business money is another outlet for my business and yours.

To get to these other profit making outlets or ideas, you have to write that book first. Once it is written, edited and formatted, there is an unlimited number of ways, outlets and income generated methods that come from that one book. Do your homework and do some research about people who have become a household name and created an empire by just one book.

If I can help, reach out to me at julia@juliaroystonenterprises.com or call me at 502-802-5385. Let's go!

Conclusion

I have three words for you, 'Write the book.'

For the final time, I am here to help you get that book written and find ways to generate income through that one book. Reach out to me at julia@juliaroystonenterprises.com or call me at 502-802-5385. Let's go!

www.ingramcontent.com/pod-product-compliance
Lightning Source LLC
Chambersburg PA
CBHW052104270326
41931CB00012B/2877